W9-BFA-301

Unexpected Shiny Things

Bruce Dethlefsen

Bruce Dethlefsen (signature)

Cowfeather press

Published by Cowfeather Press, PO Box 620216, Middleton, WI 53562.
   Website: cowfeatherpress.org
   Email: cowfeather@versewisconsin.org

Supporting materials for book groups & community reads are available at cowfeatherpress.org.

ISBN 978-0-9846568-0-6
Library of Congress Control Number: 2011939454

Cover Art: Diwas Sherchan, Author Drawing: Wilson Dethlefsen
Cover & Book Design: Wendy Vardaman

Acknowledgements

Some of these poems have appeared or are forthcoming in journals and magazines, sometimes in earlier forms. Thanks to the following editors and publications:

Anthill: "Goner"; *Between the Sheets*: "Fingernail Moon"; *Beyond Doggerel*: "Astronauts"; *Comstock Review*: "The Rest of You"; *Free Verse*: "Conversion," "Every Needle," "The House We Haunt is Ours," "Mineral Expectations," "White Stallions"; *Hands On! Drumming*: "Losing the Car Keys"; *Hepcat's Revenge*: "Fair Territory"; *Hodge Podge Poetry*: "1950," "Cross My Heart," "Nursing Home Driver," "The Opening Days," "Sewing Clouds"; *Hodge Podge Press*: "Wallpaper Faces"; *Hummingbird*: "May the Provider," "Night Sand"; *Naked Verses*: "No Wake"; *North Coast Review*: "Crows Mate for Death," "Monte Carlo"; *Recovering the Self*: "Artists"; *Seems*: "Dance Card"; *The TMP Irregular*: "The Penknife," "The Snoring Poet"; *Verse Wisconsin*: "Anniversary," "Crying Lessons," "From the Principal's Desk," "Gone to Ground," "Letter to the Editor," "Missing a Spot," "Rag and Bone," "Shiny Things," "Sixty-one," "Three-quarter Time"; *Wisconsin Academy Review*: "Apple," "I Lived Outside Myself"; *Wisconsin Game Warden*: "On the Sill"; *Wisconsin People and Ideas*: "His Name," "The Oven Clock Says 4:44"; *Wisconsin Poets' Calendar*: "First Day for Shorts," "Sleeping After Trout Fishing," "Rock My Fishing Buddy," "The Bear"; *A Wise Woman's Garden*: "The Garden is Growing Old," "Preamble to the Compost Station"; *Yahara Prairie Review*: "As the River Thaws."

"I'll Take the Moon" first appeared in the anthology *Ring Them Bells* (Mid-State Poetry Towers, 2000). "Death of My Friend" appeared in the Nekoosa, Wisconsin H.S. yearbook 1993/94.

Some of these poems were included in the chapbooks *A Decent Reed* (Tamafyr Mountain Press, 1999) and *Somewhere Near the Dance Floor* (Marsh River Editions, 2003). Thanks to these presses for the work they do.

Thanks to Wendy Vardaman and Sarah Busse, ace editors, for their encouragement and work.... and gratitude to my poetry sisters, Cathryn Cofell and Karla Huston, for proofreading. I am blessed.

May the Provider

remake me a child
near lakes trees and streams
above all awake me
from reasonable dreams

ⓢ

In memory of
Wilson "Willi" Samuel Dethlefsen
June 1, 1984 – June 9, 2010

One

Stars on Strings

On the Sill

we watch through ice stitched windows
as november covers rocks and earth
with leaves embossed with frost
that have to wait till spring for birth

the windowsill is filled
with stones that we have gathered
representing places we have known
and times that dearly mattered

so we have grown ourselves
our several rocky gardens
and now our lives connected
form and set and harden

we watch for years through sun etched windows
welcoming each freeze that kills
and thaws that will encourage
earth from which the stones emerge

we wait to be collected
on the sill

Bare Feet

all night I walk on eggshells
and it makes me cry
I thought the tears somehow
might soften up the edges of the shells

each tear drowns
the crunching sounds a bit
but the moisture helps
the smaller splinters
slide into my heels
and sink like needles in the bone

the more I walk
the more I cry
the quieter the night

The House We Haunt Is Ours

we wander through the corridors
inside the middle of the night
in little hours

I toss
she turns
we flail our arms and knees in bed
we kick at covers
spiders do the backstroke in a pool

all I need is time to write
some time to think
to get the manuscript together
I have to write better
that's the answer
writing better

she never thought she'd have no family
live unmarried
have no money
be unhappy
nuns have better sex lives

she comes back to bed and I get up
and I come back then she gets up
we alternate like this all night
shift workers at the abandoned slumber mill
the haunted house
sleepily we punch in
we punch out

separate we descend the creaky stairs
float floor to floor   swim room to room
we roam and write
check e-mail watch tv
burnt popcorn treads butter in a bowl
we stroll the blacktop
looking for our car   the keys

in the yellow lighted empty parking lot
outside the silent factory

the grinding little hours
the crawling hours
the cobweb hours
blinking in the darkness

so few words pass between us
at the gate in the chain link fence
no gestures
waves
no overtures
I whistle and I swing my lunch pail back to work
as she heads home alone to warm the bed
we haunt the little hours
that pass for night

A Vacant Lot in Guatemala

a harmony of rats and roses
fills the vacant lot next door
with music separated from the world
by walls of brown adobe

the music rises
as the roses shuffle
in the wind of the volcano
their thorns outstretched
to claw and scratch the walls

the music rises
as the rats sway
crooning in the ocean breeze
a honeyed melody
against a sky of blue and white

and each red petal falls
onto the yellow teeth of the marimba
producing notes though sweet
convey the elemental horror of the song

because all roses smell of rats
and rats of roses

(Quetzaltenango, Guatemala 1998)

Three-quarter Time
(for Rose)

I dance with you
because I can
not say the words

we change the shape
the space between
we dancers make

close in our arms
our hearts a fist
or so apart

Dance Card

the musical selections
were interrupted by the news
about our victorian neighbor
who had upped and hanged herself

of course we said
how sad too bad
it's tragic and how could she
and I thought how I'd been taught

to finish off the throw
the game the season
complete each lesson every class
hang in there
to be in it to the last
and sit enduring every play
until the curtain falls
until the death of the applause

but maybe someone else's program's shorter
not so many notes and chords before the coda
who has a small but ample dance card
listing partners filled to overflowing

one full brocaded dance card
dangling by the braided thread
as the music resumes in a cool waltz
around a blue wrist

Nursing Home Driver

her timing off
she slumps full stop
in a hallway wheelchair
highway stalled

and with her dimming headlights
tries to read and fold
her road map hands

hoping first left
then right
then left again
for any traffic
come her way

The Oven Clock Says 4:44

quick listen to the tick of it
tonight not quite
tomorrow yet my friend
the time will come
when end is ended
the light on the black
and white linoleum
no longer shines
when I am died
and done will finally
rhyme with gone

Missing a Spot

I wipe and dry the casserole dish
that fancy one with the see-through glass cover
and as I reach to put it in the cupboard
I discover I remember aunt nancy

now she's been gone forever
yet there she was
in the kitchen telling me
I missed a spot

they never really ever
go away do they

one touch recalls a thought
a thought a notion
the notion a feeling
the feeling an emotion

so then we cry or not or smile
mostly somewhere in between

and when you go
waterfall everything
will remind me of you

Not Pictured

there is a love and happiness
spirit in this pretty world's sky
and you can have me anytime

titles of the music I choose
by norman and al greenbaum
sergio mendes and boz scaggs
to be played incidentally
during a funeral scene in which
I'll not be pictured

your image pleases me
I see you step and twirl
your arms framed light above your head
whirl in turn to funeral tunes
you cry and smile
reptilian simultaneously

I picture you alive and dancing
having earned my dying gratitude
so you can have me anytime
anytime

After a Year of Being Missing

they tested the bones in las vegas
for dna and it was her brother all right
she said he'd always had the biggest dreams
I'm so sorry   we asked
was he older than you
well he used to be
but after a year of being missing
no one could tell

the bones had some effects with them
they were sure it was him
when they tested my niece and nephew for dna

now we're worried about her too   she said
frank's daughter was involved in a colt
you know
a bunch of people with crazy ideas
oh a cult we said together a cult

I knew he had gone off to die   she said
when we saw him last at gertie's funeral
I know people can just go off and die
the surprise was
that he was murdered
not really a surprise though
because I knew
he was going off to die anyway

she sealed the wadded kleenex
back in the ziplock bag on the table
and now I need some sympathy   she said

Sewing Clouds

in purple evening gown
the orange sky declines to red
I sew her name into a cloud
with needle and black thread
into the copper cloud
with needle and black thread

I purse my lips and puff a stream of air
a breeze   a sigh
to nudge it slightly
so it slides off east across the sky
out toward the hem of the horizon of the sky

in time the stitch fades from the sky
in cloud embroidery
and so redressed
her name is just another name to me
her threadbare name
is just another name to me

Grief

is salty numb cold water
come in waves
from the sadness sea

blue black heavy waves
they pound you flat
and you know the next wave
will scrunch you under
just like that
and you'll crumble into sand

so the next wave comes
to pummel you
and your knees buckle
and you are going down
done for and at least
you think thank god whomever
it's got to be over

no the next wave comes
and the next one comes
but then the waves get smaller
less often less awful
you can stand up some
and breathe a little
squeeze open your stinging eyes
hold on you can rest for a while
cause oh you'll need it
when the mourning comes

Death of My Friend

what he offered me
I hold
what he showed me
I see
what he told me
I hear
and what he gave to me
I know I know
I have

Two

⤴

Golden Coffee Sunlight

The Opening Days

the opening days
near march thirteenth
bring phenomena
on rust black wing

some fumbling
lumps of coal
start sneezing

bug-eyed
stuck in ice cream
freezing their mis er a   ble
robin asses

shudderings that barely
I mean barely pass as
springtime in
wisconsin

No Wake

go slow
no wake
ease the boat
around each corner
to a new bay

the muskrats dive
the turtles clamber
from the log
the naked bathers
scurry off the sailboat

buried

go slow
no
wait
tease the dreamy water
with your fingertips

they have to surface sometime

Sleeping after Trout Fishing

the feather fern and pillow moss
compose my bed
in sweet encomforture I doze

downstream
down stream all worry
and all water flows

my self serene
goes somewhere I suppose
drips soft
drifts off
slips out in damp repose

Mountain Dreams

you have mountain dreams
the mountain tells you bring your people

the green tongues of the leaves
say bring those you know

the blue teeth of the clouds
say bring those you never knew

the purple lips of fruit
say bring those you love

the brown mouths of the wood
say bring those who are dead

the mountain shrugs his shoulders
it's not important he says
bring who you want
we'll pile them up
dream your little dreams
it's all the same to me

The Bear

The soul is a wild animal.

—Parker Palmer

for oh so long I've sought the bear
hunted the bear
crashed the woods and pounded the bush
called the bear in my loudest voice
exhausted I sit and rest
against the oak tree
and only when I smell the shyness in the leaves
feel the roughness in the bark   the breeze
only then I see the bear approach me
snorfle my hand
and brush her paw across my chest

No Wake

go slow
no wake
ease the boat
around each corner
to a new bay

the muskrats dive
the turtles clamber
from the log
the naked bathers
scurry off the sailboat

buried

go slow
no
wait
tease the dreamy water
with your fingertips

they have to surface sometime

Sleeping after Trout Fishing

the feather fern and pillow moss
compose my bed
in sweet encomforture I doze

downstream
down stream all worry
and all water flows

my self serene
goes somewhere I suppose
drips soft
drifts off
slips out in damp repose

First Light

I thought you were birds at first
I hoped you were
yellow birds red birds brown birds

the frosted leaves fall so fast
past the barren
crab apple branches

I have failed to fill
the feeder for a week
I'm sorry

how dare you survive
without me

Lily Pads

women hate it when you say
I don't know

tell me your feelings
everyone has feelings she says
why can't you tell me your feelings

I say I think I feel

no
when you think
those are your thoughts
those aren't your feelings

doesn't she understand
that most of the time
I wouldn't recognize a feeling
if it was an alligator
that bit me on the ass

and yet

I can stand in the orange water of an autumn lake
regard the perfect placement of lily pads
sweep my hand across the dreamsicle surface
and fairly drown in feelings that are
I don't know
exquisitely okay

The Bone

men are dogs
they sing the same songs dogs do
and understand about as many words
they look this way and that way
as they eat from their bowls

they say some are trainable
they sniff at every tree to check their messages
and circle when they make their beds

about the bone   don't touch the bone
don't ask about the bone   don't try to find it
and never use the bone as a toy

men require licenses
they chase after cars and bury things
they run together to nip in play
and bite when they mean business
one bark will set off a whole neighborhood
of men all night

you can call them   they have names
like bob and lucky and lumumba
and sometimes they will come

yes there are good dogs and there are bad dogs
they constantly scratch themselves
and of course they'd lick themselves if they could
they wear collars and dig holes on hot days to lie in

you can pet them and rub them behind the ears
all you want
but remember
men are dogs
don't go near the bone
don't joke about the bone
leave the bone alone

Rock My Fishing Buddy

he's the copper cloud come to the bay
the wave that slaps the canoe
he's rude fish leather
sweat and stringy pipe smoke
oak and lily pad
he's the glad ring of water
'round the hula popper
before the strike of the bass

he's a good old hat

one last pebble bounces
on the blue skin of the drum

Conversion

I watch the autumn lake turn over
the air is colder than the water
the sun scoots on its butt across the sky
pin oak and red floating maple leaves
squeak against the side of my canoe
how can I stop this drooping of an eye
I see my breath
I smell decay
the clouds now upside down
begin to crystallize
the only way I will survive
is to invert myself
turn inside out
so my warmth comes
from within me not without
I zip my jacket up
I pierce the water
with my paddle one more time
and northward glide

Cross My Heart

don't cross my heart
I hope to die by water
not actually at the hands of water
but next to water
nearly touching the water
maybe among ferns
ferns dripping with golden coffee sunlight
that would be fine
really that would be just fine

As the River Thaws

as the river thaws
it snaps with zooming sounds
and eases up from underneath
these sudden giant footprints
open water
on a day too warm for january

another break
a moth too soon
sails over footprints flying
testing its powder wet wings
in light reflection

then the sun rolls over
on its other side to sleep
as january remembers who it is
and stomps
what's broken open
shut

First Day for Shorts

too long this winter skin
too hot this day in may
here new liver spots
there the hair
is missing from my legs
at sixty-one
an ancient ancient age
when I was young

hello knees
the both of you
the sun
the breeze

Hummingbirds

flagella move so fast
they think that hummingbirds are dead
hummingbirds know that we are dead
we mostly think that trees are dead
the trees think the water's dead
the water thinks the rocks are dead
the rocks think the mountains and the world are dead
the world thinks the universe is dead
the universe thinks that god is dead
and god who knows what god thinks

you know sometimes though
I think
I make the world go 'round
simply by walking on it
and pushing backwards just a little
with each deliberate step

The Rest of You

most of you shook out
onto your parents' graves in allouez
the rest except a tablespoon or so
I used to dust the adolescent
pepper and tomato plants
just as the sun set on the garden

that was what you told me
that was what you wished
and now I had some left

all night I worried whether I should use you
as a foot powder
so I could walk with you inside my shoes
wherever I might go
or daub you on my groin to avoid chaffing
it seemed almost appropriate

maybe mix you up with baker's clay
and form an amulet
to wear you on a chain around my neck

and while I was consumed with what to do with you
the rest of you
I spooned you with some sugar on my shredded wheat
I added milk
and ate you in a bowl of cereal

you tasted good

and that's how I'll remember you
with sprinkles

Preamble to the Compost Station

weed the peas
pull out the tomato stakes
in order to farm a more perfect onion
and radish just right

with surely mystic ability
provide formulas
mend the fence
dispose of general wildflowers

and preserve the blossoms of gardening
for our shelves and our posterity

do maintain and establish this compost station
for the beauty and sake of each miracle

and she stormed off muttering something about
pink bare legs and white panties
pink bare legs and white panties

I never told my folks

the next day I think I remember
staring at the empty bars at recess
and watching an apple with a bite out of it
roll down the blacktop past me from the jungle gym
as it bounced by in a blur I saw the hazy pink then white of it
tumbling over and over

there were many complaints about miss smootz
and I heard she'd been called to the principal's office
I'm not sure what happened there
but I remember that soon after that
girls were no longer allowed to do skin-the-cats

miss smootz must have been a real teacher
I learned so much from her

Fair Territory

when george the greek kid got goofy
and went nutso over something in our kickball game
his eyes snapped open so quick
they stretched the nostrils of his pasty face
he'd stand with one foot in fair territory
half hunched over
and clench the index knuckle of his fist
between his teeth and tug

bouncing up and down
and back and forth
the way enraged ventriloquists might fight over a dummy

when we saw that elbow flapping
we knew that george was doing his darnedest
to stifle the scream
that always followed
and that perhaps it was a good idea
to steer clear a bit
at least for another couple outs

jesus george
if only paul winchell
could hold you in his lap
just for a second
and slide one cool hand
up your back

From the Principal's Desk

bullies are unhappy people
they come from sad and sometimes violent families
where the rules change all the time
here's how to deal with bullies

ignore them   go about your business
don't feed into their unhappiness
if that doesn't work tell someone in charge
if that doesn't work travel in twos
become a friend to make a friend
if that doesn't work stand up taller
be as big as you can
bullies are cowards
holler no in their face
the bully will get smaller

respect yourself and never use violence

bullies end up lonely and alone
they'll hang around their own kind
until even they can't stand themselves
can't stand themselves

okay then   welcome back to school
it's going to be a wonderful year you'll see
with new hopes and new friends and dreams
so hey say hi to me in the hallways
and always remember the principal is your pal

Crying Lessons

you mark my words miss richards said
each one of you sometime this year
will run from this classroom in tears
some more than once I guarantee

sixth grade god hate her she was right

in january kathy hollered
holy crap my ass is bleeding
and when we laughed   we knew no better
she fled the class into the hallway

in february fred called joan a whore
we heard the choking whimpers through the door

he does or doesn't like me anymore
you're way too fat too short to be my friend
the pimples the erection the divorce
his dad her mom ain't coming home again

in march the wadded kleenex which she stored
to fill her bra inside her blouse popped out
lorraine was mortified   she and the pop
corn stopped and dropped and rolled across the floor

one by each by everyone we all succumbed

stubbornly I made it to late april
I had the flu and knew I would throw up
linda sat in front of me   her long blonde hair
from time to time would spill across my desk
I couldn't help it and I thought it best
to vomit down the inside of my sweater
I felt better right away   but fatally embarrassed
I made for the door   my tears like april rain

with permission from miss richards I had cried
at her funeral decades later how I tried I tried

Three

❧

Sifting Starlight

Every Needle
(for Mary Beth)

you say since you were little
in the christmas dark
you lay on your back
much like a present
looking up beyond each branch
each light and ornament
until you see the silver star
so far away atop the tree

gee
you are the only other
person in this world who does
and I have found you

I remember every needle

will you marry me

I want to lie with
you beneath the tree

Astronauts

at the far recesses
of space and third grade
on earth's shortest day

the astronauts shuffle out
into the moonscape playground
and seem to lift off
as snowflakes fall

rising up to the sky
bouncing weightless
against each other

dodging comets
ducking asteroids

independent of the mother ship
and mission control
in extra vehicular activity
boots kicking moon dust
mittens sifting starlight

astronauts
bundled up and
bound to explore
free floating
unfettered
the universe
untethered

at least until the bell rings

Apple

I'm sorry   she'd say to a child acting up
I thought I was the teacher here
but you must be the real teacher
and teachers must have their classroom   mustn't they
I wonder where we might find one
leading the pupil by the neck
oh here's one now

then miss smootz would tie my classmate up face down
around the base of the toilet in the bathroom
by the wrists with a towel or two
if you cry   she'd point out
you'll go to the principal's office
and you don't even want to dream what goes on
in the principal's office   now do you

one afternoon during recess
I stood fascinated
watching the second grade girls do skin-the-cats
they'd hang from the bars
throw their thin legs up between their arms
and land somehow on their feet
on the other side of themselves

upside down and almost inside out
their flowered skirts draped over their faces
they looked like they were made of rubber bands
and after a count or two they'd flip back
and resume being second grade girls again

I could watch them forever
but in a moment I was torn from the scene
pulled by the ear and marched back to the classroom
I know what you were looking at   said miss smootz
sit here and put your head down on the table
for the rest of the day
think about what you did
think hard

I Lived Outside Myself

in the steeped green and orange heat
at ten I sneaked over baking lawns
past hazy honeysuckle
between the percolating houses
seeking birds to murder in july

the birds lived out of doors
I lived outside myself

packing a slingshot fashioned
from a forked stick and surgical tubing
I pulled the pouch holding four or five bb's
back under my eye
dampened by the beading sweat on my cheek
targeting a stupid blank-eyed robin
with less than a cup or so
I judged   of life in him

he asked for it
tension and release

a butterfat pigeon tucked under
the eaves of the bubbling rooftop

he asked for it too
call and response

I slapped the life right out of them
and brewed that sun thick beverage
I poured and drank the potion
stirred sweet with the smell of robin blood
creamed white with pigeon milk

I stole their hot syrupy songs
and swallowed down july
and with my green and orange summer thirst satisfied
the tension now released
I began to live inside

Bruce Dethlefsen 55

Flowers at Risk

if somebody'll watch the baby
and my check comes in tomorrow
I can go downtown and plant some flowers
it won't cost much
and I'll still have some money left for prom
but who knows maybe steve won't even be around
and mom's no help
sure she's out but she's more interested in the bars
and at thirty-four next week
she's getting pretty tired

I'm thinking some long green vines
a couple of those spiky things
and a few petunias ought to do

just a little color
something finally growing down there
maybe between the bank and the video place
sure I know new flowers are at risk
but they're worth it
all they need is a little water and some sunshine
and somebody to watch over them
from time to time

White Stallions

the children of the street
must see themselves
in the greasy puddles of the forenoon
in the sundown storefront windows
in the luster of the shoes they shine

must see themselves
in the reflection of a customer's sunglasses
in the tears of the old women
in the shadow of the bus

the children of the street
must see themselves
flying purple kites on sunny beaches
dining with the family after church
riding white stallions

the children of the street
must see themselves

The Penknife

the day I was ten
I found a flashlight
and a penknife
wrapped inside
this note from my father
who I hadn't seen in nine years
under a rock
by the sidewalk

these are the five rules of life it said
overlight   comedy
underlight   horror
backlight   romance
no light   film noir
cut
love dad

Superglue

I superglue the splits in my fingers
they crack open and hurt me in winter

sometimes I superglue my catcher's mitt
to my left hand two hours before sunset
and superglue my dad across the street
who smells like oiled leather and cigars
under a superglued sun in the kansas city sky
to play a game of catch just one more time

I superglue my head to my pillow
that smells like my dad on an august night
in the hot and greasy kansas city night
and superglue a purple breeze to seep
through the window screen so I can sleep some

the glue fills in the breaks and stops the pain
you kids at home should not try this   refrain

Scales

the fingers of an eight-year-old fit inside
the slots between the black and white spaces
like fresh bread slices in a toaster

my father hissed and flipped a fifty-cent piece
past the piano teacher onto the keyboard

I froze in mid-scale of my second lesson

his tongue darted
he smelled the air
you should be outside
playing baseball with the other kids

he lifted me from my stool
wrapped me in his arms and squeezed
leading me away

I felt the cold shiny scales of the boa constrictor
the scales of the piano in mrs raymond's living room
where weighed in scales
I found myself wanting

the coin rolled down the keys
and came to rest near b flat
thanks he said   this is for his last lesson

with each step to the screen door
we crunched the coils of shed snake skin
into the carpet like so much dry ice

I stood sunning myself
on the sudden porch

and heard something rustle out there
shuffling among the leaves and things

Mineral Expectations

limestone awfully lonesome
since my father's gone
and miss our little talcs
gneiss conversations

how I marbled
at the strength of this good man
a grocer who would sandstone much all day
that he developed varicosities
in both his legs and never once complained

even though I took his love for granite
I can still recoal his exact words and sediments

it slate for him he'd say too late
but you shale mica difference in this world
he'd point at me and shake his finger

of quartz he understood and wished for me
not just the same old schist
but a future that pyrites
would be mined
and mined alone

The Car Salesman Hits His Stride at Fifty-five

gone are the gold tooth
the chains the medallion
the white patent leather

the day is new
I'm a salesperson
and I have something to sell
I'm a salesperson
and I will sell
sell it all

first myself
then the dream the feel
then the sheet metal

here comes the customer
remember
touch his shoulder
smile but no eye contact
be cheerful to the gourdhead
tell him what he wants
beam for the chrissake

Marrying Myself

could I revive my long dead father's heart
and touch him such that he would understand
by turning off the tv for a start
sit down with him
and ask him for my hand

explain about my honorable intentions
a plan of love in sickness and in health
connect within forsaking all conventions
engage the world
by marrying myself

with ceremony relatives and splendor
some friends and folks are laughing
someone cries
I place the ring with two doves on my finger
one dove ascending soaring   one that dies

myself I wed
united in my heart
established as my husband and my wife
I do and will until death do us part
and now begin to live and share my life

Crows Mate for Death

I know all about them
they're brilliant and greasy things
you can see it in their stare
and the way they stick together
they have fingers on the ends of their wings
but they hide them when they fly
I think they have teeth

they live forever
have you ever seen a dead one?

some of the smaller ones dress up
like blue jays and robins from time to time
I've seen the extra feathers scattered here and there
they can speak english
I heard one once in third grade
his name was jojo

a group of crows is called a murder
it's no mistake
you could look it up it's true

they're responsible for pearl harbor hiroshima
the assassination of archduke ferdinand
the failure of savings and loans
and the poisoning of our school kids with whole language

they accept donations from foreign investors
they do unspeakable things to the publicly dead
and they wait
there are so many of them
they can afford to wait

they watch me from the roadside
they know I'm not going anywhere

not really
you gotta believe me   they know all about me
crows are made for death

1950

at night
my mother bathed me in a white tub
scrubbed me with white soap
rubbed me in a white towel
hugged and plugged me
into pajamas and the white sheets

an act so kind
so common
it barely even happened

Four

❧

Unexpected Shiny Things

The Tree Story

the wind was from the west the sunset wind
it came to knock the backyard pine tree down

the tree swayed back and forth a couple times
it rocked it buckled then it snapped in three
the pine tree fell forever then the thud

the neighbors cocked their heads this way and that
at the enormous wrongness of the thing
that lay across the lawn one neighbor said
how tired it must have been and luckily
the poor tree didn't land on someone's head

I took an ax and chopped the tree by hand
the neighbor brought the chainsaw by to help
you never have to do this by yourself

we stacked the bigger logs for firewood
it takes about a year for them to dry

the stump remained I dug at it for days
exposing every root I sliced each one
and tried to pull it from the hole with chains
but every time I pulled the chains gave way
the stump's too big a job to do myself
I'll have to ask somebody else for help

my marriage grew and fell for sixteen years
I can't remember who it was yelled timber
nor precisely when but there were tears
enough to put out fires every ember

one night next june my son and I will sit
beside each other at the burning pit
he'll ask to hear the story of the tree
and how the west wind came again last summer
I'll tell him one more time what he requires
and choose another log to feed the fire

Shiny Things

I hide coins for my son to find
drop nickels 'round the playground swing
seed quarters under sawdust by the slide
place dimes beside the whirlawheel
I act surprised when he discovers
a penny along the woodchip trail
delight in the excitement on his face
his lucky smile finding unexpected shiny things

I seek objects that shine
collect and hold them in my hands
assorted coins that shimmer
crows so bright they start
the fire burning in the sky
my son his brilliant eyes
I turn them in the light
then hide them in my heart

Monte Carlo

at fourteen and a half he thinks
the future's wholly one full tank of gas

just nuts about some monte carlo
parked inside the third row
of a used car lot in green bay

the car's a two-toned job
he's told one owner
a retired polish catholic mechanic
from the chevrolet garage
who drove it only
to the packer games on sunny days
at least until the funeral
of his wife and not again

imagine dad an eighty-three
with sixty thousand actual miles
for under a thousand dollars
but they say they'll take
nine hundred cash

the boy the car
conceived and manufactured
at the same moment exactly

the cream and green boy
revved up gassed up
hitting on all eight cylinders
his eyes on high beam
braces chrome and sparkle

I smile
kick his tires for luck
pat his hood and climb on board
the father
the car
into the sun we slowly coast

A Man of the World

a skilled sewer will hand-stitch
fifty-eight baseballs
in a single ten-hour shift

my son will celebrate
the bicentennial of the civil war
and far beyond
if he can afford the parts

a chinese dissident's kidney or liver
colombian lungs
some poor ethiopian's heart

for truth he'll be a man of the world

with skin from tanganyikans
(or do they go by other names now)
a pancreas from panama
a leg from lagos
a liberian rib
an armenian arm

the cold quiet eye of eskimo

the closest I could ever come to immortality
was a five dollar japanese catcher's mitt
and a horsehide costa rican baseball
but then
I was barely alive
when babe ruth died

Evening Wear

it wasn't stealing really
I just borrowed my son's wristwatch
to wear to the board meeting

he forgot it though I thought it
was on purpose when we went back
to his mother's house on sunday
we're often late and leave in haste

I saw it right away when I got home
it had a steel blue face and golden trim
a silver twist-o-flexible band
with a golden strand that ran around it

the fit was perfect
our wrists are the same size now
although I wish the watch smelled more like him

at the meeting I daydreamed of my son
and felt the tapdance
on the ghost strings stretched between us

that night I wore my son as evening wear
the way some women
wear their man's clothes
when they're gone

my son is my accessory
I need to have him with me
and against me
bound skin to skin
manacled if need be

Goner

son I guess I'm a goner
if you're reading this my journal
my morning after morning pages
whatever for
you must be plainly curious
or maybe simply bored

did you ever have that little girl
the one I dreamed I made her laugh
does she still peek at me
from behind your knee
does she realize we're strings
stretched on the same guitar

oh well by now you probably
know it doesn't matter
but still we have to act as though it does
I hope you're publicly happy
and that if you're teaching
you're affectionate
otherwise sell tires

so I'll say goodbye son
take it easy
think about me here and there
we're father and son the same
that's why I care

How I Touch My Sons

I know how to touch one of my sons
he's such a smooth and easy touch
I watch him   listen to him
and in an instant offer up a soft and perfect touch
on his shoulder   head or thigh
without a thought

I touch him
to direct   to diagnose
to play   to emphasize
to caution   to comfort
or because his skin is hungry
or because I need the touch myself

over all these rusty years
I have managed to lose touch
and have not reached nor grasped nor held
my other son
he remains to me just out of touch
a car I cannot start in frozen morning
for lack perhaps of feeling in my fingers
or failed cold sparkplugs
beneath his skin

His Name

in the emergency ward
they said he came from the sky
by med flight helicopter
he came without a name
that's why they gave him one
xxserbia   born 1-1-1901   sex male
he was still alive

he came to me on a june afternoon
at a hospital by the river
adopted barely ten minutes old
I held him in my arms
we gave him a name
and held him for twenty-six years

I asked the doctor
please change the name
on the wristband
I can't stand it
he's got a name I said
he's willi   that's his name
he's my son
his name is willi

Gone to Ground

it takes a patch of soil
some water and the sun
to raise a plant
you make decisions
how much this and that
you feed the youngster
clear the weeds
you tend to pay attention

now there he lies   my son
fenced in and covered in the bed
his bandaged head
gauze white and crusted red
his eyes taped shut
a glut of tubes
around his nose and mouth

I make my three decisions
first no more resuscitations
save your breath   stand down
go call the donor folks
it's almost harvest time
and last at ease
unplug all those machines
please stop that awful hissing sound
what's grown so loved is gone to ground

I try to find a place
a somewhere on his face
to plant my final kiss

Sympathy Cards

go shave your face
and take your time this time
wash the dishes
dry and shelve them clean away
cut onions up
tomatoes make some chili

try and take a walk
go on the sky's still there
the clouds are full with rain
the leaves are although shaky on the trees

this world's so blue and white and green
and you still have one son left
one more son to go

Anniversary

I punch in contacts
and dial up my dead
son's phone number
as I drive by
his house on admiral
where of course he doesn't
live there any more
but cell phones are after all
miraculous devices

I park my car
and admire the lawn
green smooth clean cut
mown grass the smell
of grass just mown
the phone rings and rings
the edges of the lawn
are perfectly trimmed
how neat
how awfully admirable

Milk from Sleepy Cows
(for Willi)

here my son
today is done
the cows have all come home
drink this milk
fresh warm and silk
it's milk from sleepy cows

drowsy cows now close their eyes
to dream the orange sun down
night night cows
cream black and white
come 'round from blue green hillsides

warm and dreamy
smooth and creamy
milk from sleepy cows

rest well yourself
the world will somehow swirl
without you for a while

sleep now
deep now
not a peep now
shush boy
hush

Five

Chasing the Moon

Fingernail Moon

todos los poetas son lunáticos

we agreed that we'd look up
and find the moon to say goodnight
you at ten o'clock
me at nine
me in guatemala
you in wisconsin

I'd been tv switching back and forth
between lassie barking español
and couples calling in describing
just then
how they were making love

at nine o'clock I opened the window
and looked out past volcán santa maría
to see only low slung scratchy clouds
that smelled of yellow diesel fumes
the color of corn and the flavor of corn

so how'd it go for you

I hope you saw the moon hang in the sky
somehow tonight
if only but a fingernail
I know now why all poets are lunatics

good night

Rag and Bone
(song lyrics for *Obvious Dog*)

we wander our pathways alone
made out of rag and bone
disheveled and bruised
every crossroads we choose
wandering mazes toward home
wandering mazes toward home

rag and bone
men are but rag and bone
searching the roadways for home
this way and that way for home

each river meanders alone
swallowing stone after stone
the stick men awashed
their souls have been lost
hoping for ways to atone
hoping for ways to atone

who knows where the winds will blow
scattering seeds we sow
the sand's always shifting
the stick men are drifting
off course on their voyages home
off course on their voyages home

rag and bone
men are but rag and bone
searching the roadways for home
this way and that way for home

Sulaco Night

the end of the day
I rest
leveled by the press of sun
the rain or dust
I place
my head on the pillow
of the exhausted poet
who wrote before me
his breath
still thick in the air
his words
crawling on adobe walls
each empty space
between the words
a drop of sweat suspended
hanging in the darkness

Night Sand

I draw each moon word
in the night sand of the beach
reluctantly

I hope I never
though the tides erase all trace
lose this lunacy

Tapestry
(for the poets at St. Joe's)

regard the artistry of carp
the way they swim in woven water
doing carp wheels
down the tapestry
bump the surface
burp
then sound in deep discussion
perfect swirling circles
they descend
to bark among themselves
regarding artistry of carp

The Snoring Poet

why wake the snoring poet
while he wrestles in his sleep with words

notice as his eyelids tremble
fingers twitch as if to write
his lips about to bubble maybe burst

listen to the raspy wheeze of breath
he is a witness to the whatness unexpressed

and in the place he ought to be
where sculptors turn to stone at night
where dancers take to flight
where singers dream in harmony
and painters turn to light

please never nudge a poet snoring
cover love and keep him peace
protect him from the soundless roar of morning
let him sleep

Letter to the Editor

pathos, logos, ethos

my heart fairly breaks
for those who cannot speak
as I see hear or smell
what's happening
right here   right now
can't we do better than this
what about tradition
god knows we must protect
the future   the environment
our children   the puppies
and some kittens maybe
the cute ones anyway

Wealthy

after my reading
a very serious sixth grade girl
asked me if I was wealthy
well I said I have twenty-two
dollars in my wallet right now
my purple truck has two hundred
and thirty-five thousand miles on it
I'm wearing clean and mended clothes
I'll sleep in a warm bed tonight
I've got my health my hands my eyes
my family and friends who love me
and I can come here to sennett middle school
to read poetry to you guys for free
so yes I'm very wealthy
wealthy indeed

A Cell Phone Rings during Matthew Dickman's Reading

please answer that
no I'm serious
it may be the call
you've always waited for
the one that will
change your life forever
the one that will
make all this seem
absolutely meaningless
please answer the call
we can wait

Fruition

when perfect ripe each word falls from the limb
out of hand they splatter onto paper
it must be gravity that picks them and
helps the orchard poet in his labor

the juice runs black and shiny on the page
tomorrow words will fade and start to die
at birth all things on earth begin to rot
and smell   you can imagine if you try

though fumigated fruit may look the best
no human hand has touched except to spray
no evidence of blemish tears or sweat
no rain has washed the poison film away

please choose to use and eat bruised poems first
we who grow them know how perishable they are
and as you relish every word and verse
be sure to spit the seeds out hear and far

Laughing in the Dark

when the theater's dark
and you feel the others breathing
when the screen's asmash with light
and you hear marilyn monroe
as clear as anything sing
diapers are a girl's best friend
and you laugh so hard
you think you're gonna die
and in an instant realize
you're the only one laughing

then congratulations
shadow laugher
you're an artist
mmmm probably a poet
well maybe a critic
or dancer or painter
or sculptor maybe
but an artist
an artist for sure

How I Hang On

I've been riding whales all day
big gray whales that smell like laundry rinse
slick shiny whales
with names like lumpy rutherford and kaiser
I ride on their backs
right behind the blow hole
that's how I hang on
with my legs stretched out
almost touching their turn fins

like chill wills in dr strangelove
as he rode the a-bomb down
no   that was slim pickens
whooping it up all the way down to earth
just before everybody's bubble burst

I've been riding whales all day
big pokey bucking whales
more like merry-go-round ponies than broncos
more like roller coaster bears than fish

I saw captain ahab doing the same thing
he kept waving   kind of
as his whale went up and down
he's okay I thought
he's just taking a little nap
you know trying to get some shuteye

it's tonight I worry about
the water will be colder
the descents deeper
each sounding steeper longer
I don't know if I can hold my breath that long
I'm just not sure I can do that
and still hang on

Digital Images
(after Karl Elder)

1
queequeg's blue harpoon
guides solitary sailors
call me survivor

2
half of a sweetheart
on part of a sleeve   why did
or didn't she leave

3
emancipation
heavens and planets looming
the unfastened bra

4
poised beneath his love
cyrano de bergerac
prepares to recite

5
pregnant number one
protected from too much sun
by her sombrero

6
spermatozoan
dances and chases his tail
human weedwhacker

7
a chest retractor
allows easy access for
cardiac bypass

8
the headless snowman
developmentally slow
votes republican

9
looks like little left
on karl's guest bathroom roll
of toilet paper

0
the absence of moon
lost location of the soul
the shadow of oh

Losing the Car Keys

new drummer
that I am
I warm up and join in
skin on skin
slip into the mayhem
the rhythm and listen
I have to hear what I drum
so I can tell
which one is me

and when I find myself drumming
that's when I hear the others
and lose myself drumming
that's when we're there

that's when my hands disappear
and the drum disappears
and my car keys
tuh tuh dum
and your lover
tuh tuh dum
and even we disappear
disappear
tuh tuh dum

The Play's the Thing

a poet plays with words
the way a sculptor plays with clay
the way a picture taker
makes his thumbs a frame

the way an undertaker
plays with smiles
a poker player plays with piles
the way expectant parents
try on different names

how the drummer slaps his knees
why the beekeeper hums or not
to bees
there is no question
the artist's hardest work
is mostly play

Sixty-one

monday I crossed off cowboy
tuesday fireman
wednesday president
thursday I couldn't find the list
friday my own fishing show
saturday catching for the cardinals
sunday I took a nap
sorry
I had to
the moons flew by too soon

Wallpaper Faces

I hope someone sometime soon
is lying in bed
the coffee on the nightstand
the morning light swelling up the room
the sleeping lover draped across their chest

turning pages ever so slowly
ever so silently
abed of a whitegold morning
reading my poems
forming familiar faces
in the wallpaper
reflecting

Artists
(for Denise)

we chase the moon
too hard sometimes
and stumble in the stars

that sparkle always blinds us
we trip up tumble down
we suffocate in stardust
drown in floodlight

and still we recreate
we sing   we write
we dance   we paint
we one more time in space
ourselves remake

return   retune

gracefully we rise again
we're artists
grateful for another dreadful chance
to chase the moon

I'll Take the Moon
(for Henry Hart)

if someone will take the sun
and you say will choose water
and maybe somebody else try the earth
or love or wind
or sex or war
or fire birds or flowers
then I'll take the moon
and dedicate what's left of my life
to capture keep show and tell
utterly and complete
the epic story of the moon
but first
I need somebody to take the other things
otherwise it'll be too much for me

come on then
you take the sun
come on now
take the sun

About the author

Drawing by Wilson Dethlefsen

Bruce Dethlefsen was born in Kansas City, Missouri, in 1948 and moved to Wisconsin in 1966. He is Wisconsin Poet Laureate for 2011/2012, under the sponsorship of the Wisconsin Academy of Sciences, Arts and Letters. Previous collections include two chapbooks, *A Decent Reed* (Tamafyr Mountain Press, 1999) and *Something Near the Dance Floor* (Marsh River Editions, 2003). *Breather* (Fireweed Press, 2009), his first full-length book, received an Outstanding Achievement Award in Poetry from the Wisconsin Library Association. Twice-nominated for the Pushcart Prize, Bruce's poems have been featured on Garrison Keillor's *The Writer's Almanac* and *Your Daily Poem*, where he was Poet-of-the-Month. Bruce also performs original music with Bill Orth as *Obvious Dog* on Cathryn Cofell's CD, *Lip*.

His son, Nathan, lives in West Salem, Wisconsin. His other son, Wilson, died in a moped accident in June, 2010. A retired educator and public library director, Bruce lives with his partner of twenty years, Sue Rose Allen, in Westfield, Wisconsin.

He still believes the flying dreams are the best.

About the publisher

Cowfeather Press is a project of *Verse Wisconsin,* an independent, mission-driven, print & online magazine located in Madison, Wisconsin. If you are interested in learning more about Cowfeather, or how you can support this fledgling effort, email cowfeather@versewisconsin.org; visit Cowfeather Press, cowfeatherpress.org, and *Verse Wisconsin,* versewisconsin.org; follow *Verse Wisconsin* on Facebook, where news of Cowfeather also appears; or contact us by mail, Cowfeather Press, PO Box 620216, Middleton, WI 53562.

Supporting materials for book groups & community reads are available at cowfeatherpress.org.